Carolyn Jackson

If I Had A Dog

Illustrated by

France Brassard

Tundra Books

Published in Canada by Tundra Books,
75 Sherbourne Street, Toronto, Ontario M5A 2P9

Published in the United States by Tundra Books of Northern New York,
P.O. Box 1030, Plattsburgh, New York 12901

Library of Congress Control Number: 2005927008

Library and Archives Canada Cataloguing in Publication

Jackson, Carolyn, 1943-
     If I had a dog / Carolyn Jackson ; France Brassard, illustrator.

ISBN 0-88776-725-7

     1. Dogs–Juvenile fiction. 2. Picture books for children.
I. Brassard, France, 1963- II. Title.

PS8619.A25I3 2006   jC813'.6   C2005-902894-7

We acknowledge the financial support of the Government of Canada through
the Book Publishing Industry Development Program (BPIDP) and that of the
Government of Ontario through the Ontario Media Development Corporation's
Ontario Book Initiative. We further acknowledge the support of the Canada
Council for the Arts and the Ontario Arts Council for our publishing program.

ONTARIO ARTS COUNCIL
CONSEIL DES ARTS DE L'ONTARIO

The illustrations for this book were rendered in watercolor on Arches paper.

ISBN-13: 978-088776-725-8
ISBN-10: 0-88776-725-7

Printed and bound in Hong Kong, China

1 2 3 4 5 6   10 09 08 07 06 05

For Maxine and Hugh,

and in memory of Lucky, Pal, Mitzi, Piper, and Gracie.

- C.J.

To my dear mother

who always believed in me.

- F.B.

Maxine loved dogs. Her family didn't have one, but Maxine wished that they did. She watched dogs. She followed dogs. She dreamt about dogs. She collected stuffed toy dogs, china dogs, dog clothing – anything to do with dogs, until the house was full of every kind imaginable. Every kind, that is, except the living, breathing kind.

Maxine was sure that problem was solved when a friendly black dog came right up to her on the street. He was all alone. Naturally, she took him home.

"Mom," she said. "Look at him. He's lost. He wants to live with us forever." Maxine held on tight to the dog's collar so he couldn't escape.

Mom looked at the dog. "Maxine," she said gently, "he is wearing a collar and a tag. He seems well cared for and healthy. I think he already has a home."

Maxine's dad read the tag. "There is a phone number here," he said. He dialed the number and spoke. "Yes, we have your dog. . . . He's fine. . . . Sure, you can come for him right now."

Five minutes later a lady rushed in and hugged her dog. "Oh, thank you," she said. "I don't know how my Piper got out of the yard, but we're so lucky you found him!"

The lady took Piper home.

Maxine sat on the front steps and watched them go. She was discouraged. "Piper would have been perfect for us," she told herself. "And anyway, if I had a dog, I would make sure he never got lost."

Maxine's brother, Hugh, came out. "Mom said we could walk to the park, Maxine. Let's go and play for a while," he said, trying to cheer up his sister.

As they passed their friend Sarah's house, she called to them. "Come in and see what we have." Sarah's dog, Molly, was inside with four new puppies.

"Please be careful," Sarah's mom said. "Dogs are very protective of their babies. They can get upset if people come too close or disturb them. Just talk softly and watch for a minute or two, but don't touch."

Outside, Maxine said, "If I had a dog, I wouldn't want her to have puppies because I wouldn't be able to keep them all, and that would be sad." Hugh agreed.

As they walked along, Maxine and Hugh saw a woman with a tiny dog on a leash. Maxine darted toward it.

"Stop, Maxine!" Hugh warned. He remembered what he had learned when his class visited an animal clinic. "You should ask the lady if you can pat her dog. If she says yes, walk up to it slowly and calmly," Hugh said. "Then stretch out your hand and let the dog sniff you. After that you can pat him. Patting on the shoulder is best."

Maxine followed Hugh's instructions and patted the little dog gently.

The lady smiled and said, "Thanks for asking. My dog, Gus, is very small. He is afraid of getting hurt when people run at him. When dogs think they are in danger, they sometimes growl or even nip to protect themselves."

When they were walking again, Maxine said, "If I had a dog, he would never be afraid because I would always be there to keep him safe."

On their way past Morgan's Garage, a big dog barked and jumped up behind the fence that surrounded the repair yard. They stopped to watch as Mr. Morgan came toward the fence.

"Hello, you two. I heard the noise and came to see what was happening. Lucky is here to guard the property, and he's barking to tell you to keep out. It's best if you stay back because he could get angry if he thinks you are trying to come in without permission."

Maxine and Hugh moved on. "If I had a dog," Maxine said, "I wouldn't make him guard anything. We would just play all day."

At the corner, a man with a dog in a harness stood waiting at the curb. "Let's go and ask if we can pat that dog," said Maxine.

Hugh was pleased that Maxine had remembered to ask, but the man said, "It's a good thing you checked first, because my dog, Pal, is working. Since I can't see, I depend on him to help me get around the city. He has to concentrate on traffic and obstacles – all the things that might be a problem for me. Please don't interrupt him while he is working. I give him lots of pats and hugs when we are at home." The light turned green and Pal led the man safely across the street.

"If I had a dog," said Maxine, "it would be as smart as Pal. I just know it."

On the way past the fruit and vegetable store, Maxine and Hugh noticed a dog tied to a pole. "Poor thing," said Maxine, "she's all alone. Let's keep her company."

A lady who seemed to be searching for the perfect peach said, "That's my dog, Mitzi. Like you, she knows enough to be careful of strangers. When dogs are tied up, they can feel threatened and try to protect themselves. I wouldn't want Mitzi to growl or scare you, but since I'm here now, you may certainly touch her. She knows I would never let anyone hurt her."

When the lady went back to her peaches, Maxine whispered, "If I had a dog, I would never leave her tied. I would take her everywhere with me."

At the park, Maxine and Hugh played on the slide, and Hugh even pushed Maxine high on the swing until she was laughing and dizzy. When her stomach felt too full of butterflies, they played catch with Hugh's baseball.

All of a sudden two lively dogs that had been chasing each other around the park raced up and snatched at the ball. They almost knocked Maxine down. She was a little frightened.

"Stand still, Maxine, and look away. They won't want to play with you if you don't move." Sure enough, the dogs calmed down and Maxine and Hugh walked quietly away. The owner returned the ball, apologized, and put his dogs on their leashes.

"If I had a dog," Maxine said, "of course I would let him play with his friends, but I wouldn't let him run wild where children were playing."

Maxine and Hugh came to a bench where two people were having a chat. Each one had a dog. One dog was chewing on a bone.

"I'd like to pat your dog," Maxine said.

"It would be better to wait till Gracie finishes eating," said the man. "If you put your hand near her head now, she might think you are trying to take her bone away. She wouldn't like that at all. Gracie takes her food very seriously."

"May I pat your dog, then?" Maxine asked the lady.

"Yes, dear," said the lady, "but wait just a minute. My Bonnie has dozed off. She is getting old and sleepy, just like me, and her poor joints are aching. I don't think she hears very well anymore, either. If you touch her while she is sleeping it will startle her. I'll wake her very gently first."

"It's all right, don't wake her up," said Maxine. "Maybe she should rest."

"If I had a dog," Maxine whispered to Hugh, "I'd make sure she had lots of bones and a lovely soft bed so her legs wouldn't ache."

As they neared the bike path, Hugh shouted, "I'll race you to that tree over there!" He already had a head start on Maxine. She chased after him. Just then, a big dog lunged at a boy who whizzed past on his bike. The dog's teeth were bared and the hair on his back was standing up. Luckily, the owner had control of his pet and pulled him back.

Hugh remembered what the veterinarian had taught his class. "If ever you meet an angry dog, you should fold your arms across your chest and stand still. If the dog is staring at you, you shouldn't stare back. Look at the ground and be quiet. Don't run, even if the dog sniffs at you. If you are calm, the dog might leave."

"If I had a dog," said Maxine, "I don't think he would ever be angry. He'd be happy all the time because I would love him so much."

"Do you even know how to tell when a dog is happy?" asked Hugh. "I do. Happy dogs wag their tails and sometimes their whole bodies wag and wriggle. When dogs are happy," Hugh continued, "their tongues might flop right out over their teeth and they might open their mouths to pant. They look kind of like they are laughing. Some happy dogs stretch out to lick you or smell you, and some bow down to invite you to play."

"If I had a dog," said Maxine, "he'd be so happy, I bet his tail would wag right off!"

"You know, Maxine, your dream dog might be perfect, but the truth is, you don't *have* a dog!" Hugh sighed. "For your information, neither do I, even though I wish I did every bit as much as you."

Maxine frowned. It was more fun imagining she *did* have a dog. If her brother wanted one so much, why couldn't he pretend too? Maxine dragged her feet all the way home.

Their mom met them at the door. "You two must have enjoyed yourselves. You were gone so long, I was about to come looking for you," she said. "Let's go into the family room and see what Dad has in there."

Maxine and Hugh followed their mom. At the doorway, Maxine's eyes nearly popped out of her head. Even Hugh was amazed. There in a corner, all curled up in a nice soft bed, was a wriggling, tail-wagging, tongue-lolling puppy!

"We thought you might like a little surprise," said Dad laughing at their faces.

Maxine and Hugh were thrilled. "We'll take good care of her," promised Hugh. "We've been practicing all day!"

Maxine agreed. "But Dad! Mom! How did you guess we'd be so happy . . .

. . . if *only* we had a dog!"